The Youngest Ocean

The Youngest Ocean

Christopher Cessac

WAYWISER

First published in 2018 by

THE WAYWISER PRESS

Christmas Cottage, Church Enstone, Chipping Norton, Oxfordshire, OX7 4NN, UK
P.O. Box 6205, Baltimore, MD 21206, USA
https://waywiser-press.com

Editor-in-Chief
Philip Hoy

Senior American Editor
Joseph Harrison

Associate Editors
Eric McHenry | Dora Malech | V. Penelope Pelizzon | Clive Watkins
Greg Williamson | Matthew Yorke

Copyright © Christopher Cessac, 2018

The right of Christopher Cessac to be identified as the author of this work
has been asserted by him in accordance with the
Copyright, Designs and Patents Act of 1988.

All rights reserved. No part of this publication may be reproduced, stored in
a retrieval system, or transmitted in any form or by any means, electronic,
mechanical, photocopying, recording, or otherwise, without the prior permission
of both the copyright owner and the above publisher of this book.

9 7 5 3 1 2 4 6 8

A CIP catalogue record for this book is available from the British Library

ISBN 978-1-904130-94-9

Printed and bound by
T. J. International Ltd., Padstow, Cornwall, PL28 8RW

for Marie, Adras & Etta

Acknowledgments

Borderlands: Texas Poetry Review: "Valentine, Texas."

cant: *"Six Characters in Search of an Author* in the Wal-Mart Parking Lot," *"Lives of the Poets* at the PTA meeting" and *"Leaves of Grass* inside McDonald's Playland."

Confrontation: "Troy, Montana."

Drunken Boat: "Loving, New Mexico" and "Eve, Missouri."

Legal Studies Forum: "Ophelia, Virginia," "Solomon, Alaska," *"Women Poets of Japan* at the YMCA Swimming Pool," *"Your Cheating Heart* on the morning commute," and *"Zen and the Art of Motorcycle Maintenance* at Jiffy Lube."

The Modern Review: "The Youngest Ocean."

Mudlark: "Homer, New York," "Milton, Louisiana," *"Beyond Good and Evil* on date night," *"Ars Amatoria* in the express checkout lane," *"Me and the Devil Blues* at the Chamber of Commerce luncheon," and *"Midsummer-Night's Dream* in baggage claim."

Sub-Lit: "Keats, Kansas," "Sappho, Washington," and "Clio, South Carolina."

32 Poems: "Ovid, Michigan."

Valparaiso Poetry Review: "Romance, Wisconsin."

Poems in Section I, The Oldest God, previously appeared in the chapbook *Eros Among the Americans* (Main Street Rag).

Contents

Foreword by Andrew Motion   13

I. THE OLDEST GOD

Amor, Minnesota   17

Troy, Montana   18

Keats, Kansas   20

Loving, New Mexico   21

Laura, Ohio   22

Ovid, Michigan   24

Homer, New York   26

Valentine, Texas   28

Clio, South Carolina   29

Arcadia, Iowa   30

Sappho, Washington   31

Eve, Missouri   33

Broken Arrow, Oklahoma   34

Ophelia, Virginia   36

Solomon, Alaska   37

Milton, Louisiana   38

Contents

Romance, Wisconsin   40

Josephine, Alabama   41

Eros, Arkansas   42

II. FOLK, SONGS, ETC.

Six Characters in Search of an Author in the Wal-Mart Parking Lot   45

Lives of the Poets at the PTA meeting   46

True love at home
   (to the tune of *Love in Vain Blues* or *Robinson at Home*)   47

Your Cheating Heart on the morning commute   48

The Origin of Species, kindergarten graduation   49

Midsummer-Night's Dream in baggage claim   50

The Tale of Cupid and Psyche and the county fair   51

True love is secretly stealing from work
   (to the tune of *Statesboro Blues* or *The Idea of Order at Key West*)   52

Beyond Good and Evil on date night   53

Me and the Devil Blues at the Chamber of Commerce luncheon   54

True love connects through DFW like the rest of us
   (to the tune of *A Sailor Being Tired* or *Wish for a Young Wife*)   55

Women Poets of Japan at the YMCA Swimming Pool   56

Contents

Zen and the Art of Motorcycle Maintenance at Jiffy Lube	57
True love is down to earth, totally normal, really, like one of us (to the tune of *O Death* or *Huffy Henry hid the day*)	58
True love needs overdraft protection (to the tune of *Goodnight Irene* or *La canción desesperada*)	59
Leaves of Grass inside McDonald's Playland	60
Ars Amatoria in the express checkout lane	61
True love is both late and early (to the tune of *Little Glass of Wine* or *To An Athlete Dying Young*)	62
How should I your true love know from another one? (to the tune of *Little Maggie* or *Mad Girl's Love Song*)	63
Poetics in the Suburban	64
La Vita Nuova in a box on the moving van	65

III. THE YOUNGEST OCEAN

The Youngest Ocean	69
A Note about the Author	81
A Note about the Anthony Hecht Poetry Prize	83

Foreword by Andrew Motion

Elizabeth Bishop, when asked what criteria she used to judge a poetry competition, said with characteristic deprecation, "I just want to be surprised". And so say all of us. However we interpret the word surprise – which, after all, has meanings that range from wonderful to nasty – we know that our pleasure in a poem has a great deal to do with startlement. Not necessarily the shock of receiving an idea that is entirely unheard-of, but the thrill of recognising something we had forgotten we already knew. The surprise of confirmation, in fact – which then might well become the foundation for ideas that we have not previously considered.

These kinds of pleasure abound in Christopher Cessac's collection *The Youngest Ocean*, and seem all the more remarkable because their power to affect us in primitive human ways (by stirring our strong feelings, by amusing us, by intriguing us) cannot easily be separated from their strongly literary character and interest. That's to say: they deploy a compactly witty style, they make a multitude of more-or-less learned references, and they play all manner of cerebral games, but they never lose their common touch. In this respect they remind us of T. S. Eliot's judgment that "thought" to John Donne was a form of "sensation".

Take the first third of the book, "The Oldest God", in which a number of (real, existing) American towns and smaller communities that are named for historical figures, several of them mighty and dead poets, become the locations for a fragmentary narrative of love and belonging. In the process, small town America is incorporated as the site of feelings that mingle – in a profoundly familiar way - the lofty with the humdrum. "Keats, Kansas" gives a good example of how the sequence works, as it looks for consolation among the contradictions of desire:

> ... *half in love with Easeful death,*

    half in love with ephemeral ecstasies of living:
    sex and parades and wisdom. Others need us

Foreword by Andrew Motion

> we hope as off we go into the tumor
> I mean world to wrestle I mean embrace.

The second section of the book, "Folk Songs, etc", elaborates these procedures by similar means. In doing so, it simultaneously deepens the impact of the earlier poems and spins their themes into new directions – sometimes totally straight-faced, sometimes wistful, sometimes almost farcical. The character of the narrator that emerges from this (as it were) mirror-ball diversification is often at a loss: "I too, a mere tender of machines/and mortal as the rest, tend to destroy all/that I don't understand. As with rain or romance/it will always seem to be too late or too soon". In this respect, as in all other human shows the series makes, we are constantly reminded of what is familiarly confusing and mortal, while also being entertained by the dazzle of the poems' performance.

The final third of the book is a single long poem, the title poem of the volume, and modifies the preoccupations of its two earlier parts into a more obviously political form. The arrival of Columbus in North America; the consequences for language; the impact on our sense of geography (what lies beneath physical surfaces and what is imposed upon them); the legacy of imposed social structures and prejudices: all these and more are swept together in the draft of the poem's progress, and all are handled – as we might expect, given the dexterities of the work that precedes them – with a very likeable mixture of gravity and lightness.

The Hecht Prize is a distinguished thing, and *The Youngest Ocean* is a distinguished winner. As well as providing a wealth of surprising pleasures in the here and now, it whets our appetite to read whatever Christopher Cessac will write in the future.

I.

THE OLDEST GOD

Amor, Minnesota

Call us pioneers. We're most sincere
when we lie. Gods and goddesses, perfect

bodies dipped in nectar and longing
for us . . . We feel deceived and our own

deceptions thus justified. Ordinary bones
and how life unrolls, never quite secure

from loneliness. Every love deserves a temple.
We long to sing of inexpressible things

lovelier than beauty. But days race and language
is rarely so resilient or inventive as evil.

Troy, Montana

Having found the ecstasies of flowers
and fruit bring worms, insects, so much

hurt, some trees will choose to stand
bare and alone. We will always be unhappy

lovers—trying to set fire on fire.
Something west pulling us, Last Chance

Gulch to here, to learn again
even mountains have a lowest point.

To want you yesterday
as evergreen red cedars must

want the stars last night—the past
keeps us. A great divide

and a long highway back
to Helena. Most beautiful,

most everything, most, most . . .
Youthful judgments hunt us forever.

The old wish for youth, not years.
By love we mean confuse. Take pity on us,

nothing is left to take. Confuse us. Take war,
for example, every war, and leave. Blooms,

berries, that pageant of sex and birth
made sense once—we were young and wise,

drunk on greed and good wine we saved
too long. Vinegar, bare trees. Winter

Troy, Montana

is a thing we each face in our own way.
Do you sleep alone? The loneliness

we find in others can be a great comfort.
Troy was not undone in a day. The small

and quiet blows that build and build.
A great divide and a long highway back.

Keats, Kansas

Not for lack of love but because of too much
we grow furious. This year's malignancies

responded well and spread nonetheless.
The fall will bring festivals and parades

to avoid. Love comes naked and hungry, in need
of comfort. Despite the climate, despite the work,

there can be comfort—some nights a little sex
between nightmares, some mornings the wisdom

to see in contradiction a means to truth: as pain
is to joy and so on ... *half in love with Easeful death*,

half in love with ephemeral ecstasies of living:
sex and parades and wisdom. Others need us

we hope as off we go into the tumor
I mean world to wrestle I mean embrace.

Loving, New Mexico

Let that burning wheatless dust spit gas at us
and let the more efficient tend to their just-soiled

dinnerware—who faced with eternity
would not tremble? Let the temperate grovel

in our wine-soaked mud, let flowers come
by armful to decent old lovers—no horror or joy

unsettles us now. Let it burst or collapse,
the whole world, its rose petals and grease traps …

The doors locked, our limbs knotted, in love
with love—let them all burn slow with envy.

Laura, Ohio

If I could tune my sighs to such gentle music as Laura makes
—Petrarch

To hate everything you hate—what love
ever promised more? Food, rest . . .

Necessity demands too much. The ideal
versus the living, with all their screeching,

their stench and negligence. Hair, name,
anything can be changed: a muse

has no say in these matters. Early reports
could be wrong, maybe there is nothing

but anticipation. Beg life for love, beg love
for peace. War, suicide—to amuse ourselves

we'll try everything once. Twice, we left
Laura, gathered our ancient notions

of romance and thrift and found work
on a line in Lorain. Just before sleep,

it hits us: only one short life. By morning,
we forget. The sun abandons others

who need it more and perhaps know
what to make of it and rises east

of Laura. Sun, don't lecture us
about modern man, his soul

and its heart-shaped hole.
We desire what can never be.

Laura, Ohio

Why want less? The collected muses
of world literature understand us.

We are not malicious. We mean
to help. We don't. We can't.

Ovid, Michigan

What we need is a prayer for lovers
neglected too long. Brutal thugs

have had their way with us; romance
deserves a turn. I know everything

anyone wants to know about love
and studying the moves of famous lovers

is not the way. Learn from my mistakes.
Of course only the wise and happy can love

and only love brings wisdom or happiness.
A good florist in East Lansing is good

to know if you're going to a funeral. Lovers
are seduced by mystery and excitement

not botany, not merchandise. And not poetry.
Find a lost soul scribbling rhymes

and you've found one who truly loves
failure. The goal is to be loved

not loveable and they are not the same.
A movie in Saginaw. Dancing in Lansing.

A picnic at Lake Ovid is not the worst idea.
But never twice. A romance demands to be

dependably new. And a picnic
at Lake Ovid is as good as any other

time to realize you've been doing everything
wrong until now. I only understood

Ovid, Michigan

how much was at stake when I noticed
even the enemies of love in love.

Homer, New York

Homer, one more Greek Revival
off Main Street will be the answer

to what? Doric columns, two stories, etc.
For whom? One more Jedediah or Hannum

pork-barreling mercantile fantasies,
a horse trade then another, an extra

capital gain, another lost cause, one more
more—because, children of Homer, because.

Should we abandon our meager libraries
to laws and liturgies? What the past suffered

is cause for rebellion. We're all veterans
of a too familiar war: all tomorrows

versus the next moment. Stop. Come,
anywhere, maybe a drive down

to Virgil, slow through ice and wind,
the car radio desperate to bring us

comfort and comfort is good—
even our thick heads grasp that much

on occasion. Occasionally, to prove
there's nothing extraordinary about us,

we do just as our ancestors: we choose
from among the most successful gods

and call it faith or love or fate. Less myth
than rumor, a brutal alphabet of grunt

Homer, New York

and groan and howl, the smallest sounds
that can pass for truth—a slim volume

from any library: Horace or Sappho
or Hank Williams, all tomorrows

or the next moment. Stop. Consider
ancients in Scandinavia who sang of gods

fighting chaos and evil to the end
despite understanding their destiny

was to fail before chaos and evil. Homer,
those were rare gods worthy of our love.

Valentine, Texas

That intimacy between cruelty and love
can seem at times too obvious. Still, it's hard

to be a French Decadent Poet in the desert
towns of West Texas. Maybe Saint Valentine could

find something to love among the ruins. Like music,
like discontent, like old friends sharing a bottle

and the moon, regret and desire circle
the town. The young flee from beauty

and call it pursuit of beauty. Voluptuous
torture, sublime torment—beware

of common-sense. Surrounded by nothing
but dust and sun and yet drowning.

Clio, South Carolina

Enough furniture and enough years
you can call any place home. Exile

saves most of us—an elsewhere useful
or well-governed and there time to be

entirely. Some wise pleasure-loving god,
classical and vague, would understand

nothing of the drywall and bluster
that lets a town pass for a town. Music

is enough but there is never enough music.
Our children, fresh from the war, defenseless,

remind us that a brief skeleton of happiness
is at least happiness of a kind. Stagger back

to a life lived between apathy and pathetically
shaking a tiny fist. Historians, ignore us,

please—competent malcontents, unfamous
lovers—we have no history, only a past.

Arcadia, Iowa

A peaceful life in an unwalled city.
Beautiful nymphs frolicking in a lush forest.

Do we ask too much? Oblivion
for one moment might be enough.

The city was killing us. We fled
to the countryside. But we had killed

the countryside already. We forgot. Our god
we made from a goat: a rustic jumble of Saint

Peter and Pan. No war, no labor,
no sorrow—defining happiness

by absence, by negation. Forget last night
or at least tomorrow. Without forgetting,

what life could be endured? Good company
and a song or two is all I have to offer

but if you bring some wine then wine
is ours to share. Bring love

and there will be love too. The peacock
and peahen don't ask our permission,

let's not ask for theirs. And if the morning
glories refuse to bloom until we sober up,

let them. Jealous morning glories.
Tired of being in this world

doesn't mean tired of being. Oblivion
for one moment. Do we ask too much?

Sappho, Washington

Aphrodite [
                    ] only god [   ]
these endless battles [
        ] and the black earth [
        ] to be your [
        ] comrade [
and lightly [
            ] is all

    . . . .

   ] desire [

   ] the devout will always find a temple
[
   ] bright stars made brighter [
   ] one glimpse [   ]

    . . . .

[   ] glaciers [

   ] again the struggle of salmon [
   ] pathetic [

   ] Clallam County Fair [   ] monotony
   ] refuge of the library in Fork [

   ] delicate neck
        ] close to me and [
        ] life delicious [   ]

Sappho, Washington

. . . .

[   ] like us [

        ] refuse [
        ] threadbare [
        ] unintelligible [
        ] almost [
        ] lost [
    ] music found [

                                  ]

and more than life [

                ] deserves [   ]

Eve, Missouri

Shortness of breath, quickening heart—
language falls short, sex never looks good

on paper. O ye gentle retired bureaucrats,
disgruntled playgirls, whistleblowing-wanna-be

toadies, join my song. For we have loved
both youth and style—the usual

mistakes of our time. The Latter Day Saints
may be right: the Garden of Eden is in Missouri

if it's anywhere. Frozen for months, for months
hot as anywhere. Only the cruelest beauty for us.

Brutal and graceless youth, we know so little
of pleasure. So much pleasure is lost on us.

Snakebite, blizzard, cancer, head-on collision:
how many reasons does love need? Desire

is fig leaves, the unknown. Familiar fruits
can satisfy at times but never wholly satisfy

our longing for complaint. To separate
darkness from light requires light and darkness.

Endless pleasant weather—who could bear that?
Ask any retired prime mover or romantic

meteorologist, the importance of storms, collisions,
of fevers and bites, something, not too much,

just enough to pique desire—
if such a thing can be measured.

Broken Arrow, Oklahoma

Overwatering redbuds, neglecting rose beds—
what could the neighbors possibly know

of love? Still you demand proof
that gods reward evil. Always

so many of us in the room
we never thought of ourselves

as lonely. All those husbands
and wives that were not ours,

all those that were. Broken Arrow,
pronounced thlee-Kawtch-kuh. Cupid,

they walk right on the moon. Science
reveres nothing. The countless stars

counted, named and classified.
An almost plausible philosophy

to bring sleep or reasons for one night
would change everything. Vague hallucinations

guide us: praise literature but leave the books
to accountants, pledge allegiance to romance

but our only ritual is languor. Feigning
helplessness, watching as the unlovable

take all the love. In a landlocked land,
we manage to be islands. As islands,

we manage to find something like comfort
beneath a blank, black sky. No moon or stars—

Broken Arrow, Oklahoma

their grace and promises and lust recall
too much disappointment, too few good years.

Cupid, will there be rewards for endurance?
Will there still be something like endurance?

The only lust left is lust for gratitude
as gratitude has become our surrogate for grace.

Ophelia, Virginia

The world would rather rest than move
without purpose but a purpose is easy

to come by. Appetites compel us.
What was so compelling? Here we are

but who can remember. Romance or mercy,
what we can we take. Wicomico, Chesapeake,

Potomac—loyalty or nostalgia has kept us close
to water. Closure or what passes for closure.

To love in moderation is useless. No dictionary
gets it half right. A lover bears the world

by imagination—contemplating horrors
and how they magnify without you in it:

even beside you, I long to be beside you.
Useless moderation, what we can we take.

Solomon, Alaska

A summer narrow and rude and cruelty
inspires too much. Yes, the birds and bees

left years ago. No one followed. No one
blamed. Who doesn't owe and deserve

an apology? The New American Standard
Version of King James on King Solomon:

song of songs—dove-eyed, goat-haired,
honey-tongued, better than wine. Almost.

And recent history is gold or at least lust
for gold: no town, boomtown, ghost town,

same as everywhere. Winters are sudden
and then always. Long screams of wind

that shift and shove and swing. So much ice
reminds us to love something. Almost.

Milton, Louisiana

We lie to our young. Exiled
from calm, only motion remains

to define us. Glorious dust,
even tragedy escapes us.

Milton Volunteer Fire Department,
have mercy upon us and protect us—

hammering out of our owne hearts,
as it were out of a flint, the seeds and sparkles

of new misery to our selves,
till all were in a blaze againe . . .

The Argument: you—half-full glass
of wine, a Byzantine halo gold

as any god—maintain skies dull as mud
might rain, then bright blossoms, etc.,

the overbearing allure of life . . .
Rebuttal: I—a cause for everything, at once

efficient, material, formal, final—conclude
Luke got this right: *there shall be weeping*.

Mammon and Moloch throw the best parties,
agreed, but so much of life crawls or darts

beyond our perception. Wisdom? Years and age
bring blindness. Enter a Chorus of Angels:

"Limitations of space forbid full disclosure.
Trust us." Recall the motion of puppets,

Milton, Louisiana

villains and heroes, the rush and lag of youth . . .
Recoil, serpent, a glistening live oak

in Louisiana is no more alone
than the rest of us. Romance

has always been our best opportunity
for tragedy—*falling between worlds and worlds*—

hand in hand with wandring steps and slow . . .
close, closer, mud against mud,

unendurable grace of pure desire. *Easier
than air with air*. A familiar myth retold

endlessly: knowledge, the fall, blah, blah,
a burlesque of death and life, of potential . . .

These too-measured portions of happiness
versus the infinite we long to deserve.

Romance, Wisconsin

We keep poor records. What matters most
happens so slowly no records are kept at all.

Sad, not tragic. The evidence against romance
grows weak with the years, as years gain strength.

Unpaintable beauty versus all those millions
of paintbrushes and still paintbrush factories

are busy as ever, even now, even as we lie
to sleep. Venuses and Cupids, mere children

of salt and dust, parading lust and want, flaunt
a promise of desire that only fools the young

and the old and especially the middle-aged.
There are times the world and I get along

and times this North Fork of the Bad Axe
River is not just enough, but too much.

All that remains now of Romance
is the Romance Tavern and its buffet.

Old age, work, marriage, children—
Romance was abandoned for the usual reasons.

What matters most happens so quick no records
are kept at all. Call it coincidence, convenience

or romance, but this valley cutting quietly
through forest could be excuse enough

for now, for us. There are so few reasons
to be alone and there is so much night.

Josephine, Alabama

In the beginning was appetite.
A slender conceit: good farms fat

with kindness and desire.
A word like fruition is enough

to discourage most of us.
Self-love, self-hate, what else

are we expected to try? The enemy
is always near, fumbling

through a quiver, blind or drunk
or both, overcome with lust

or vengeance or both. Beauty
complete in an incomplete world:

the hurt and thrill of each day
slowly into past tense—memory

and appetite. Assume everything ends
as it begins, with only chaos

and desire. A word like fruition
expects too much.

Most of what we are up to
will never resolve.

Eros, Arkansas

A radio singing for us. Eros
reminisces on a long career—

alone in someone else's kitchen
and something like a well-worn guitar

or is it fresh fruit and whiskey
on the table and of course love

was still in its bohemian stage: beauty
with room and time to grow

and all of this understood in terms
of poverty, by what we lack.

II.

FOLK, SONGS, ETC.

Six Characters in Search of an Author in the Wal-Mart Parking Lot

The day begins as parody of a day beginning.
Our children gather for the arts (martial

as usual). I still know how to find a good deal
of trouble. Confusing life with plot and how

to construct a decent one. The descent one makes
into fictions: this lust-filled convenience of on and off

ramps as we roam village to village in search
of necessities: a bargain on bliss or at least good

beer. Bare of music, waiting in the wings, still
no script with parts for us, half-heartedly rubbernecking

with my herd, the last good music I heard
left me and that was it. What is it you do?

See how sometimes I please and/or harm others?
That's all I do.

Lives of the Poets at the PTA meeting

A desire for beauty did not lead to this.
Long before birth, all we wanted from life

was too well known, too bluntly limned
in glorious vulgarities, all gusto and cocksure

heroic verse. At times we need cruel kings
to blame, a convenient excuse, something

to expedite the scenery. A call to order, a second
and adjourn. The prized game ball long deflated, dust

on trophies with gilded figurines doing those things
no longer done—we remember too well the education

we never had. I too, a mere tender of machines
and mortal as the rest, tend to destroy all

that I don't understand. As with rain or romance
it will always seem to be too late or too soon.

True love at home

(to the tune of Love in Vain Blues or Robinson at Home)

Everyone agrees this wants a name
other than love—bucolic hurricane, toxic

anodyne, something, anything the boys
in marketing can run with. To sleep with

a hypothesis is to miss the physical joy
of a life lived. Deadlines, beginnings,

which wakes you? Tomorrow Luminal
or the blues, regrets, scruples. Today

woo, mollycoddle, cavort, swap spit, frolic
and spoon. Well-armed with the latest in lust

and nothing's good or evil but always
a bit of both. Addicted for now

and now is so much. We all shill
for something, why not romance?

Your Cheating Heart on the morning commute

Consider parades you have known: patriotic,
funereal or otherwise, versus the occupation

of the moment and what each heart can bear.
The motion, at least, satisfies. Hank warbles

timeless anachronism through subwoofers
of satellite-fed hope. Into that space

that you would still call heaven, contrails
ease onto the morning's long, clean canvas

but I have no plane to catch. Along the highway,
the harvest has given way to fields of stubble

burning. I'm no farmer. Within that space
you would still call a soul, somewhere between New

Orleans and old age, money still explains too much.
Consider all the parades we never knew.

Zen and the Art of Motorcycle Maintenance at Jiffy Lube

A moment to romanticize pathetic fallacies
of the old technologies—moods of cities, love

of cameras ... Technology now is not just
sleeping with your first wife, handicapping

greyhounds or scanning our old books, it's here
in the waiting room. A life among mechanics,

quantum or otherwise, and this morning's acting
manager-on-duty can render abstract the concrete,

oil-stained floor with a wave of his smartphone.
Dumbstruck, our laptops lapse, and we wait.

The manager knows this poem like most needs more
sex or wisdom; he understands too well our machines

and how ungenerously they repay our affection,
how little we do but wait; how little else we can.

True love is down to earth, totally normal, really, like one of us

(to the tune of *O Death* or *Huffy Henry hid   the day*)

Our parents were wrong. About the future,
democracy, marriage, art. So much happens

only when we're young. Without a god or drugs
or with a variety of gods and very good drugs—

we deal with death. We don't have a choice,
there it is: open-mouthed, stiff, glass-eyed,

gone. Our parents were young, probably. In love
and right about everything. Music, gambling,

bad jokes, good food. About sharing it
with someone wise and unappeasable

enough to—just when this modest war
against infinite loss demands action—

scale the neighbor's aging sycamore and fill
this gray street with an angry, sweet song.

True love needs overdraft protection

(to the tune of *Goodnight Irene* or *La canción desesperada*)

>Don't be too proud of your songs,
>loverboy. An executioner may be
>
>humming one prettily at work.
>Another may be deemed best-suited
>
>to push next year's widget.
>Remember pathetic Orpheus,
>
>pulled by grief to hell itself,
>his music moved even death
>
>to tears but zilch
>to show for it.
>
>And yet, to sing still,
>knowing it could win him
>
>nothing.
>That was the first love song.

Leaves of Grass inside McDonald's Playland

If not preparing to die, living is what
then implies each deodorant commercial

voiceover and gaudy sunset, each cold
CAT scan all summer like insects abuzz

with feeding, breeding, mad larval days
romanticized to the point of tragedy. Farce

begins like this—a complete loss. *Lose the tie*
a wise warm drawl had cautioned in vain.

Manhatta, *something specific and perfect* against
the usual music of exhaust and ember. To end

among these strangers and miles from warmth
or pulled-pork barbecued nostalgia—as if home

might be adopted, as if adapting were enough.
Beards grow as we wait. Lines form. Hearts slow.

Ars Amatoria in the express checkout lane

Everything—love, lust, even our alphabet—
was young once. If only to amuse death

we should have paused more for photographs.
Or less. Having reduced their immediate desire

to ten items or less, the young lovers before us
in line remind us of blameless lives our mothers

and doctors dreamt for us before these small crimes
that we call a career—the romance of life

in our provincial outpost is no romance. Eros,
that deathless, heartless god of hearts, taught us

to make our own sweet trouble by abandoning
us as he abandons all in time. Our time alone

together: a lucky marriage of sweat and song,
life held close, with purpose, if only to amuse death.

True love is both late and early

(to the tune of *Little Glass of Wine* or *To An Athlete Dying Young*)

That the beautiful is difficult is too small
a reason to settle on the picturesque. No art—

a little poem especially—has room enough
for even one short life much less the subtle

grievances and varied pleasures of a romance
complete. It makes for splendid theatre:

dying young, in love and all of the world
against us. For us, the world has mostly been

indifferent. The difference, we blundered
into noting, is of that gravity and grace

to be revealed in love old and weathered.
Consider today's news from the expedition:

a pair of skeletons enfolded. Last kiss or clutched
in fear? No difference, professor. No difference.

How should I your true love know from another one?

(to the tune of *Little Maggie* or *Mad Girl's Love Song*)

If the stars still exist there is no proof here.
A sleepless hum and glow, the incandescence

of arrogant, adolescent streets.
Confusing the littlest dulling of desire

for the opposite of love,
we desert each other too soon.

Crazy Horse understood
the ancient stars above

the Black Hills ordering themselves
as a great Thunderbird means a thaw

is coming, with blooms and promises,
but also a terror of lightening,

a razor of wind, ceaseless rain.
Senseless to expect one without the other.

Poetics in the Suburban

Parked. Idling. Oblivious to the weather
or whether the crops are in, what the factories

are paying, when the troops are returning. Aristotle
would understand. These moments are hard won

and fragile. A little selfish space to dwell
on the precious—iambs (a life?), the introduction

of scenery (this parking lot?), the difference
between Comedy and Tragedy ("the comic mask

is ugly and distorted, but does not imply pain").
This is the natural order of things. To cower,

at times, from all responsibility, to give
the heart a rest as smooth as sleep. To wake

and find the lot is full, the vultures circling,
pained expressions, coveting my space.

La Vita Nuova in a box on the moving van

Sing the fixed mortgage and all-night pharmacy
and Spring's fresh layer of asphalt to smooth

the lot between the liquor store and sushi place.
Sing in our coarse native tongue; the local muses

don't speak Latin anyway. One way we misspent
the decade was postponing our efforts. Exports

and interest rates weigh less now, thank God,
thank Buddha, thank peat-smoked single malt.

A single fault to point to? Who cares. Music
feels good again and that alone is almost enough.

Most of life is reflection; ironic given how little
time there is to live. A thousand dances, a lake

of whiskey and a million kisses ago, we knew
muses are mortal and the best songs unfinished.

III.

THE YOUNGEST OCEAN

The Youngest Ocean

Nothing beautiful to say about the world
and never stop trying to say it.

A sense we've known happiness before
so there can be happiness. What happens

depends. How to be in this world
and what role model doesn't disappoint.

A desire to persist despite. Everything
before and how it relates to what is possible:

as Columbus is the name of no one
long before trombones and flags parade

down Fifth Avenue in Manhattan—
a King's army retreats, King's College

is rechristened Columbia University—
The Manhattan Project begins in secret

and never ends—Japan is *Cipangu,*
where Columbus believes he will arrive—

. . . .

Start with an impossibility of art:
This world does not exist—everything just

as possible as nothing. Don't trust literature.
Poets too can camouflage selfish reasons

for killing others like the rest of us.
It's not easy being President,

finger on the button, etcetera.
Before our wars, before even happiness:

the entire sprawling suburban log-cabin
penthouse empire of convenience,

even invitations to the inaugural ball,
unlikely as life itself . . .

               . . . .

               Water
and no horizon—creation stories
begin like this (an exhausted albatross,

a ball of fire after a fleeing serpent,
a boy fishing who lands an island,

the sun sprouting from an egg)—
names, details vary, but first: water.

And even water loves to hear its name
so we name:
               Atlantic, after Atlas,
from our catalog of sensibly absurd heroes
punished with unbearable chores—

How many ways to say it, our one myth:
resistance is useless.
               For Prometheus
sunrise is knowledge a beak will knife

into his stomach again, every morning
is both life and dread . . .

The Youngest Ocean

               Tantalus
encircled by, yet wanting, olives,
figs, a pomegranate, a single drop
of water . . .
           Sisyphus with his rock
and Camus his pen to push and push . . .

Adam and Eve and being made to live
with death . . .

          Atlantic, after Atlas,
the weight of any heaven is on a man's back.

      . . . .

*. . . in order that the crew might not be dismayed
if the voyage were long . . . two reckonings:*

*the smaller which was false
and the greater which was true.*

      . . . .

Any honest cocktail party and some crude
academic with no contempt or sympathy

for empire will yelp of Leif Ericson
and Vikings finding old, unknown shores—

"District of Leif"?
         It lacks romance,
sounds like conquest or shipwreck,
not discovery; his story, not history.

      . . . .

The Youngest Ocean

Interbrand, a division of Omnicom:
*[W]e developed the name Prozac. This abstract
name cleverly combines the positive
associations based on the Latin/Greek
derivations of 'pro' with a short, effective
sounding suffix. ... Brands are an important
influence on our lives. They are central
to free markets and democratic societies.*

. . . .

Not Interbrand, Congress or cartography,
"Columbia" is developed within a poem:

*Where e'er Columbia spreads her swelling Sails:
To every Realm shall Peace her Charms display,
And Heavenly Freedom spread her golden Ray.*

by Phillis Wheatley, a slave—existence
is not simultaneous: the speed of light

versus the sloth of heavenly freedom
and her rays; the sunlight we know is years

older than now—each morning both life
and dread, a world old and unknown.

. . . .

A war knows the work of secrets
and how to bury them—
                                Beneath bleachers
at Stagg Field, a vacant stadium turned arena

for gladiators in gray flannel, labcoats, egos,
anxious, hurried to prove The Bomb can be.

The Youngest Ocean

. . . .

Stagg Field, after Alonzo Stagg—
All football comes from Stagg,

says Knute Rockne: the huddle, numbers
on jerseys, tackling dummies,
                                the shift
in focus from defense to offense and surprise:

hidden balls, criss-crosses, reverses, laterals;
it's Stagg who introduces the forward pass—

fourth down, fourth quarter, desperation,
who wouldn't throw a bomb?

. . . .

Stagg Field and a squash court turned lab—
a chain reaction in uranium lets loose

an impromptu celebration: cheers and chianti
in paper cups follow a quick call to D.C.

to whisper the agreed-on secret phrase
announcing success:
                        The Italian navigator
has landed in the New World.

. . . .

Too much sake and dancing, the moon
and cherry blossoms have conquered

Capitol Hill, I'm drunk, reeling from poems
you've whispered, secrets the Secret Service

The Youngest Ocean

will never hear . . .
                How to be in this world
and even against unbroken suffering, beauty
and peace are pursued still, if only to argue—

. . . .

Climbing the mast to look for land
or landing at Columbus International:

On one hand: charity, our neighbors, their children,
what happens to this world after us.

On the other: our own comfort (a full belly,
some wine, a solid roof, a soft place to fall at night).

Each moment we prioritize and live.

. . . .

If revolution is equal parts philosophy
on fire and cold muscle of desperation

then America was never revolution.
To write a winning creation story

demands discretion: no Pemaquidians,
no Pophamites, no bullion-hungry shiploads

of Roanokers abandoned to die on islands
off Carolina's coast, no godless aristocrats

lusting for Spanish gold, for real estate,
for fortunes in salt-slacked cod shipped

from Maine for decades before Plymouth.
Forget all these.
                     Start with honest Pilgrims:
worship and work, worship and work—

and Squanto waiting for us, grateful
to work our crops, worship our gods . . .

            . . . .

Interbrand: *strong brands bestow value
far beyond the performance of the products
themselves. Brands that do this possess an idea
worthy of consumer loyalty.*

            . . . .

                     Loyal and clever,
well-placed, well-read—always others,

eager, busily repainting Pentagons, *War*
departments into *Defense* departments

to not announce a shift in focus, a leaning
toward empire—
                 Calliope or We
the People, Polyhymnia or polycarbonate
conglomerates, we all have our muses . . .

            . . . .

George the Third: *I wish nothing but good,
therefore everyone who does not agree with me
is a traitor and a scoundrel.*

The Youngest Ocean

Bush the Second: *The reason we start
a war is to fight a war, win a war,
thereby causing no more war.*

Roosevelt the First: *In strict confidence ...
I should welcome almost any war,
for I think this country needs one.*

Nixon: *I'd rather use the nuclear bomb ...
Does that bother you? I just want you to think
big.*

. . . .

    Our little freedoms, what should we do,
flaunt them? To what end? Some illiterate,

treeless outpost on the Black Sea?
Ask Ovid the pleasures of such a reward.

So what then? Fetch the boss's laundry,
bang away at one more *Aeneid*? It's not easy

not being President: someone else's finger
on the button, etcetera.
                    Capitol Hill,
Fifth Avenue, the Interbrand board room—
so many ways to measure distance between us

and none adequate—a ghost town in Morocco,
a landlocked village off the Black Sea . . .

What should we do? Settle down, forget
the future, reduce the world to what we can

hold?—some olives, a few pomegranates,
a lover, our children. Pastoral dreaming

solves everything except what matters.
Fellow exile, to not be present is not enough.

. . . .

Ovid: *I'm punished because my unknowing eyes
saw an offence, my sin's that of possessing sight.*

For what, naming names? *Carmen et error?*
Exiled and here at home, among my own.

How else to explain shame at seeing the flag
over there and over there and over there . . .

Columbus the wise proving the world
is round, Pilgrims and Indians embraced

in Thanksgiving, *in order to form
a more perfect union, of the people, created

equal,* etcetera. What do you expect
from a schoolboy—I believed it all.

Centuries pass. Cemeteries and landfills fill
to near bursting. What do we do?

We grow old. Find work. Try for love.
The alternatives are too grim.

. . . .

Columbus on *Santa Maria* or Tibbets
on the *Enola Gay* or Balboa curled up

The Youngest Ocean

like a dog, hiding beside his dog
in a barrel on a boat headed west,

or General Curtis Lemay, fast in battle
like a lion, or Captain John Smith, unwearying

master of guile and toil, or De Soto, Octavian,
Truman, *certaine Knightes, gentlemen, marchanntes*,

Honest John, Davy Crocket, Pershing,
Ajax, Hercules, Fat Man, Little Boy . . .

    . . . .

Atlas tending his garden of gold
at the western limit of the known world.

A hero arrives, asking only for rest.
Are you secure enough to let some stranger

loiter among everything you have?
Atlas refuses.

    So the hero offers a gift
and who is so satisfied as to refuse a gift?

Atlas is staring as the hero raises the head
of Medusa. First his feet, then his legs—

Atlas becomes a mountain, clouds scratch
his stone shoulders, on his back falls

the work of keeping heaven
separate from world and men.

    . . . .

The Youngest Ocean

There have always been many ways
this world could end; it's beginnings

that escape us. Empire or people
resisting empire . . . What could be more

valuable than a new world, everything
before versus what is possible—

. . . .

Two hours after midnight land appeared . . .
green trees . . . fruit of various kinds . . . naked people

. . . in order that they might feel great amity
towards us, because I knew they were a people
to be delivered and converted to our holy faith
rather by love than by force, I gave to some
among them red caps and some glass beads
. . . and many other things of little value.

A Note About the Author

Photograph: Steven S. Miric, 2018 ©

Christopher Cessac was born in 1967 in Corpus Christi and grew up in South Texas. He studied literature and history at Texas A&M, law at the University of Michigan Law School, and poetry at Johns Hopkins University. He has worked as a writer, musician and lawyer. He lives now in Toronto. His first poetry collection, *Republic Sublime,* won the *Kenyon Review* Poetry Prize. He is also the author of *Eros Among the Americans*, a chapbook, and his poetry has appeared in *The Antioch Review, Black Warrior Review, Cimarron Review, Drunken Boat, Kenyon Review, Poetry Daily, Rattle,* and elsewhere. One of his poems introduces *Rio Grande*, an anthology of prose edited by Jan Reid and including work by Larry McMurtry, John Reed, Américo Paredes, Woody Guthrie, Molly Ivins and others.

A Note About the Anthony Hecht Poetry Prize

The Anthony Hecht Poetry Prize was inaugurated in 2005 and is awarded on an annual basis to the best first or second collection of poems submitted.

FIRST ANNUAL HECHT PRIZE
Judge: J. D. McClatchy
Winner: Morrie Creech, *Field Knowledge*

SECOND ANNUAL HECHT PRIZE
Judge: Mary Jo Salter
Winner: Erica Dawson, *Big-Eyed Afraid*

THIRD ANNUAL HECHT PRIZE
Judge: Richard Wilbur
Winner: Rose Kelleher, *Bundle o' Tinder*

FOURTH ANNUAL HECHT PRIZE
Judge: Alan Shapiro
Winner: Carrie Jerrell, *After the Revival*

FIFTH ANNUAL HECHT PRIZE
Judge: Rosanna Warren
Winner: Matthew Ladd, *The Book of Emblems*

SIXTH ANNUAL HECHT PRIZE
Judge: James Fenton
Winner: Mark Kraushaar, *The Uncertainty Principle*

SEVENTH ANNUAL HECHT PRIZE
Judge: Mark Strand
Winner: Chris Andrews, *Lime Green Chair*

EIGHTH ANNUAL HECHT PRIZE
Judge: Charles Simic
Winner: Shelley Puhak, *Guinevere in Baltimore*

A Note About the Anthony Hecht Poetry Prize

NINTH ANNUAL HECHT PRIZE
Judge: Heather McHugh
Winner: Geoffrey Brock, *Voices Bright Flags*

TENTH ANNUAL HECHT PRIZE
Judge: Anthony Thwaite
Winner: Jaimee Hills, *How to Avoid Speaking*

ELEVENTH ANNUAL HECHT PRIZE
Judge: Eavan Boland
Winner: Austin Allen, *Pleasures of the Game*

TWELFTH ANNUAL HECHT PRIZE
Judge: Gjertrud Schnackenberg
Winner: Mike White, *Addendum to a Miracle*

THIRTEENTH ANNUAL HECHT PRIZE
Judge: Andrew Motion
Winner: Christopher Cessac, *The Youngest Ocean*

Other Books from Waywiser

POETRY
Austin Allen, *Pleasures of the Game*
Al Alvarez, *New & Selected Poems*
Chris Andrews, *Lime Green Chair*
George Bradley, *A Few of Her Secrets*
Geoffrey Brock, *Voices Bright Flags*
Robert Conquest, *Blokelore & Blokesongs*
Robert Conquest, *Penultimata*
Morri Creech, *Blue Rooms*
Morri Creech, *Field Knowledge*
Morri Creech, *The Sleep of Reason*
Peter Dale, *One Another*
Erica Dawson, *Big-Eyed Afraid*
B. H. Fairchild, *The Art of the Lathe*
David Ferry, *On This Side of the River: Selected Poems*
Daniel Groves & Greg Williamson, eds., *Jiggery-Pokery Semicentennial*
Jeffrey Harrison, *The Names of Things: New & Selected Poems*
Joseph Harrison, *Identity Theft*
Joseph Harrison, *Shakespeare's Horse*
Joseph Harrison, *Someone Else's Name*
Joseph Harrison, ed., *The Hecht Prize Anthology, 2005-2009*
Anthony Hecht, *Collected Later Poems*
Anthony Hecht, *The Darkness and the Light*
Jaimee Hills, *How to Avoid Speaking*
Hilary S. Jacqmin, *Missing Persons*
Carrie Jerrell, *After the Revival*
Stephen Kampa, *Articulate as Rain*
Stephen Kampa, *Bachelor Pad*
Rose Kelleher, *Bundle o' Tinder*
Mark Kraushaar, *The Uncertainty Principle*
Matthew Ladd, *The Book of Emblems*
J. D. McClatchy, *Plundered Hearts: New and Selected Poems*
Dora Malech, *Shore Ordered Ocean*
Jérôme Luc Martin, *The Gardening Fires: Sonnets and Fragments*
Eric McHenry, *Odd Evening*
Eric McHenry, *Potscrubber Lullabies*
Eric McHenry and Nicholas Garland, *Mommy Daddy Evan Sage*
Timothy Murphy, *Very Far North*
Ian Parks, *Shell Island*
V. Penelope Pelizzon, *Whose Flesh is Flame, Whose Bone is Time*
Chris Preddle, *Cattle Console Him*
Shelley Puhak, *Guinevere in Baltimore*
Christopher Ricks, ed., *Joining Music with Reason:*
34 Poets, British and American, Oxford 2004-2009

Other Books from Waywiser

Daniel Rifenburgh, *Advent*
Mary Jo Salter, *It's Hard to Say: Selected Poems*
W. D. Snodgrass, *Not for Specialists: New & Selected Poems*
Mark Strand, *Almost Invisible*
Mark Strand, *Blizzard of One*
Bradford Gray Telford, *Perfect Hurt*
Matthew Thorburn, *This Time Tomorrow*
Cody Walker, *Shuffle and Breakdown*
Cody Walker, *The Self-Styled No-Child*
Cody Walker, *The Trumpiad*
Deborah Warren, *The Size of Happiness*
Clive Watkins, *Already the Flames*
Clive Watkins, *Jigsaw*
Richard Wilbur, *Anterooms*
Richard Wilbur, *Mayflies*
Richard Wilbur, *Collected Poems 1943-2004*
Norman Williams, *One Unblinking Eye*
Greg Williamson, *A Most Marvelous Piece of Luck*
Greg Williamson, *The Hole Story of Kirby the Sneak and Arlo the True*
Stephen Yenser, *Stone Fruit*

FICTION

Gregory Heath, *The Entire Animal*
Mary Elizabeth Pope, *Divining Venus*
K. M. Ross, *The Blinding Walk*
Gabriel Roth, *The Unknowns**
Matthew Yorke, *Chancing It*

ILLUSTRATED

Nicholas Garland, *I wish ...*
Eric McHenry and Nicholas Garland, *Mommy Daddy Evan Sage*
Greg Williamson, *The Hole Story of Kirby the Sneak and Arlo the True*

NON-FICTION

Neil Berry, *Articles of Faith: The Story of British Intellectual Journalism*
Mark Ford, *A Driftwood Altar: Essays and Reviews*
Philip Hoy, ed., *A Bountiful Harvest:*
The Correspondence of Anthony Hecht and William L. MacDonald
Richard Wollheim, *Germs: A Memoir of Childhood*

* Co-published with Picador